4/12

D0605406

DISCARD

AMAZING INVENTIONS

PHONOGRAPH

MARY ELIZABETH SALZMANN

Consulting Editor, Diane Craig, M.A./Reading Specialist

Sandcastle

An Imprint of Abdo Publishing
abdopublishing.com

abdopublishing.com

Published by Abdo Publishing, a division of ABDO, PO Box 398166, Minneapolis, Minnesota 55439. Copyright © 2016 by Abdo Consulting Group, Inc. International copyrights reserved in all countries. No part of this book may be reproduced in any form without written permission from the publisher. SandCastle™ is a trademark and logo of Abdo Publishing.

Printed in the United States of America, North Mankato, Minnesota

062015
092015

THIS BOOK CONTAINS
RECYCLED MATERIALS

SAN JUAN ISLAND LIBRARY
1010 Guard St.
Friday Harbor, WA 98250

Editor: Alex Kuskowski
Content Developer: Nancy Tuminelly
Cover and Interior Design and Production: Mighty Media, Inc.
Photo Credits: Wikimedia, Shutterstock

Library of Congress Cataloging-in-Publication Data

Salzmann, Mary Elizabeth, 1968- author.
  Phonograph / Mary Elizabeth Salzmann ; consulting editor, Diane Craig, M.A./Reading Specialist.
    pages cm. -- (Amazing inventions)
  Audience: Grades PreK-3.
  ISBN 978-1-62403-710-8
  1. Phonograph--Juvenile literature. 2. Inventions--History--Juvenile literature. I. Title.
  TS2301.P3S28 2016
  621.389'3--dc23
                          2014045327

SandCastle™ Level: Transitional

SandCastle™ books are created by a team of professional educators, reading specialists, and content developers around five essential components—phonemic awareness, phonics, vocabulary, text comprehension, and fluency—to assist young readers as they develop reading skills and strategies and increase their general knowledge. All books are written, reviewed, and leveled for guided reading, early reading intervention, and Accelerated Reader™ programs for use in shared, guided, and independent reading and writing activities to support a balanced approach to literacy instruction. The SandCastle™ series has four levels that correspond to early literacy development. The levels are provided to help teachers and parents select appropriate books for young readers.

EMERGING · BEGINNING · TRANSITIONAL · FLUENT

CONTENTS

ALL ABOUT PHONOGRAPHS

Thomas Edison invented the phonograph in 1877.

It is also called a record player. It plays recorded sounds.

5

The first records were **cylinders**.
They were made of tin.

Flat records were
invented in the 1890s.

Old record players have handles.
Turning the handle plays the music.

Newer record players don't have
handles. The record turns by itself.

A needle runs over the record.
The sound comes out of the horn.

Speakers replaced horns in
the 1920s. The sound comes
out of them.

Today music is on **CDs**.
Jay listens to a CD.

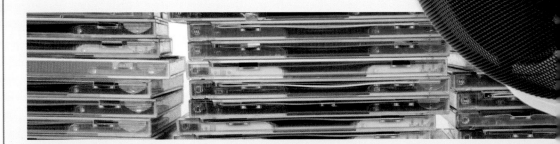

POWER   REPEAT

PROGRAM

TRACK   PLAY/
PAUSE

PROGRAM   CD DISPLAY   REPEAT

SKIP/SEARCH   STOP   PLAY/PAUSE   SKIP/SEARCH

AM — 53   60   70   85   110 140 170 x10KHz

FM — 88   92   96 100 104 106   108 — MHz

LOG SCALE 0 • 1 • 2 • 3 • 4 • 5 • 6 • 7 • 8 • 9 • 10 LOG SCALE

◄ TUNING ►

Music is **digital** too. Computers and phones can play music.

Angie plays her favorite song.

THINK ABOUT IT

What music do you like?
How do you listen to it?

GLOSSARY

CD – a round plastic disc that music or computer files can be stored on. *CD* is short for *compact disc*.

cylinder – a solid, round shape with flat ends. A soda can is a cylinder.

digital – able to be used on a computer, or using computer technology.

replace – to put something new in the place of.

speaker – a device that changes electrical signals into sound.